Presidential Elections

All About the Electoral Process, Campaigning. Political Parties, and Much More!

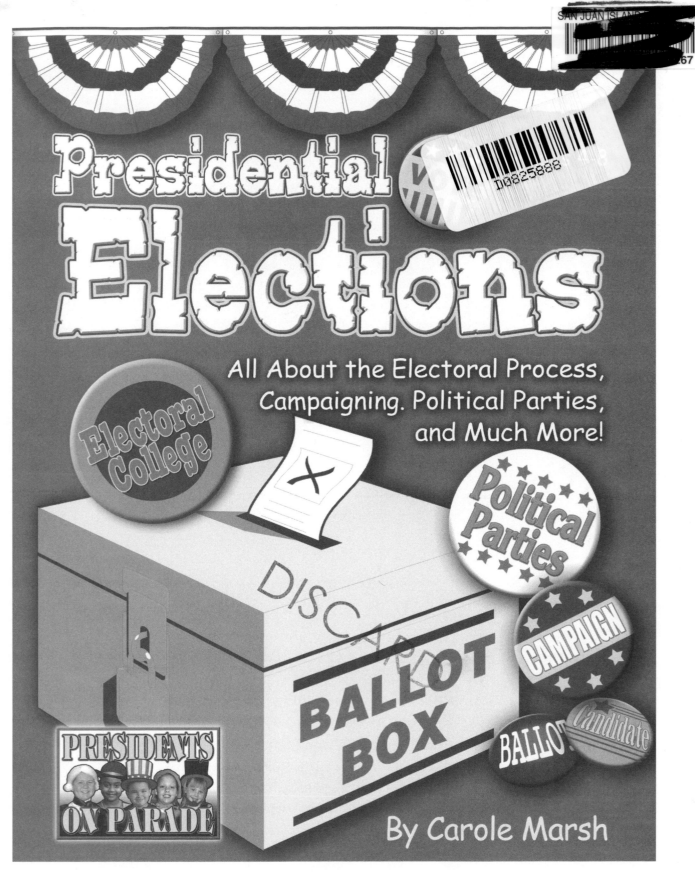

Electoral College

Political Parties

CAMPAIGN

BALLOT BOX

DISC

BALLOT

Candidate

PRESIDENTS ON PARADE

By Carole Marsh

Editor: Chad Beard ● Graphic Design: Cecil Anderson & Lynette Rowe ● Cover Design: Victoria DeJoy

1

Published by

GALLOPADE™
INTERNATIONAL

800-536-2GET
www.gallopade.com

Gallopade is proud to be a member of these educational organizations and associations:

The National School Supply and Equipment Association (NSSEA)
American Booksellers Association (ABA)
Virginia Educational Media Association (VEMA)
Association of Partners for Public Lands (APPL)
Museum Store Association (MSA)
National Association for Gifted Children (NAGC)
Publishers Marketing Association (PMA)
International Reading Association (IRA)
Association of African American Museums (AAAM)

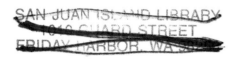

Other Carole Marsh Books

Presidential Readers

George Washington
Father of Our Country
By Carole Marsh
1000 READERS #1

Abraham Lincoln
Great Emancipator
By Carole Marsh
1000 READERS #5

Thomas Jefferson
Man of the People
By Carole Marsh
1000 READERS #7

James Monroe
Author of the Monroe Doctrine
By Carole Marsh
1000 READERS #13

Ulysses S. Grant
Unequaled Union General
By Carole Marsh
1000 READERS #20

James Madison
Father of the Constitution
By Carole Marsh
1000 READERS #23

Woodrow Wilson
World Peace Champion
By Carole Marsh
1000 READERS #65

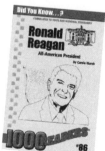

Ronald Reagan
All-American President
By Carole Marsh
1000 READERS #86

Jimmy Carter
The Nobel Prize President
By Carole Marsh
1000 READERS #107

Franklin Delano Roosevelt
President With a "New Deal" for America
By Carole Marsh
1000 READERS #92

Dwight D. Eisenhower
President & Five Star General
By Carole Marsh
1000 READERS #100

John Adams
America's Second President
By Carole Marsh
1000 READERS #122

John F. Kennedy
America's Youngest President
By Carole Marsh
1000 READERS #110

Theodore Roosevelt
America's "Rough Rider" President
By Carole Marsh
1000 READERS #127

Andrew Jackson
The People's President
By Carole Marsh
1000 READERS #125

3

A Word From The Author

For more than 200 years, Americans have had something to get excited about — presidential elections! From George Washington to George W. Bush, we wonder and wait — and often work very hard — to see who will be elected the next leader of the United States.

You may be wondering why I would choose to write a book like this for kids who are not old enough to vote yet. There are several reasons why I wrote this book for you:

1. America needs you! That's right, YOU are America's future. And the time to get ready to make your special contribution as a citizen is NOW. Everything you learn in school will help you become a responsible citizen in your city or town, county, state, and nation. You don't have to be 18 to help out with elections, so pay attention!

2. Public service is an honorable occupation. While you might hear adults complain about "elections," the democratic form of running America is famous around the world. Citizens in other countries give their lives so that their homeland can have democratic elections. Many Americans have made the same sacrifice. It's up to you to be sure that they did not die in vain.

3. Elections and politics are not hard to learn about. They are not boring. Both are fascinating, fun, and will be part of your life all your life, so you might as well plan on participating! Good government is what *you* make happen, not what happens to *you*.

By the time you finish this book, I hope you will see your opportunities to be part of the dramatic enterprise we call the United States presidential elections. And, I hope you will be excited about the who, what, when, where, why, and how of presidential elections! I hope you're looking forward to becoming a voter — your vote counts!

Carole Marsh

Who Can Vote?

The United States would have no state or local government if the voters did not elect other people. This single fact should make you see why people make such a big deal out of elections.

No one should ever take voting for granted. After all, once upon a time, even in America, not everyone could vote. For a long time, African Americans and women were not allowed to vote.

In colonial times, people voted "Yea" (yes) or "Nay" (no) with their voices. Today, we go to a poll, which may be a school or other public building, to vote on a ballot which we might fill in by hand or select our favorite candidates on a computer.

To be able to vote, you have to be eligible and then you have to register. But none of this matters if you do not get out of bed, get dressed, and go to the poll on Election Day and vote!

If you can answer "yes" to all of these questions, you can (and should) vote!

REGISTRATION FORM

	YES	NO
1. Are you at least 18 years of age?	☐	☐
2. Are you a citizen of the United States?	☐	☐
3. Are you a resident of this state?	☐	☐
4. Do you have a clear record? (No felonies)	☐	☐
5. Are you of "sound mind?"	☐	☐

Fast Fact!

Each state has similar rules regarding voter registration, however they are not all the same. (North Dakota does not require voter registration at all!)

5

The Life of the Party

It is very important that you do not feel like "the government" belongs to someone else, or is someone else's responsibility. This is *your* government. *You* are the government.

You don't have to be rich or famous to run for office. You have to be eligible, and you have to file. Then, if you want to, you can campaign for that office by getting out and talking to people and letting them know how you feel about things and what you can do for them.

The main way we elect people to public office in the United States is through political parties. You can join a political party. This may be the Democratic Party, the Republican Party, or one of the many other parties which exist. You can also vote as an "independent" which means you don't belong to any particular party, but just vote for the person you think will do the best job, no matter which party they may belong to. (There is also a political party called the American Independent Party, and other "third parties" arise, then disappear, from time to time.)

I think I'd like to be a:

_____ Republican

_____ Democrat

_____ Vote independently for whomever I want to.

_____ Belong to the _____ Party

I think I'd like to:

_____ Work to help someone else get elected to public office

_____ Run for public office

6

Fast Fact!

A new political party will often revolve around a political personality. For instance, Theodore Roosevelt had been a popular Republican president. In 1912, Theodore Roosevelt and his followers formed the Progressive Party, or Bull Moose Party. The name came from Roosevelt's reply when a reporter asked how he felt. "I feel as strong as a bull moose!" he said.

Political Parties!

The two major political parties, the Democratic and Republican parties, dominate the electoral process. Both major political parties are organized to win elections, control government, and influence government policies. Each major political party seeks to define itself in a way that wins majority support while remaining committed to its core principles.

Number the steps necessary to become a politician.

_____ You are nominated by your party.

_____ You join a political party.

_____ You decide to get involved in government.

_____ You talk to friends and family about running for office.

_____ You participate in debates and talk to voters.

Put a checkmark by each positive way to get involved in your government.

_____ 1. Vote.

_____ 2. Write to your congressperson about an issue that concerns you.

_____ 3. Complain to your friends and neighbors about the mayor.

_____ 4. Join Mothers Against Drunk Driving.

_____ 5. Send nasty voice mail messages to your congressperson.

Fast Fact!

Don't celebrate yet! The word "party" comes from a French word meaning "to share."

Who Can Become President?

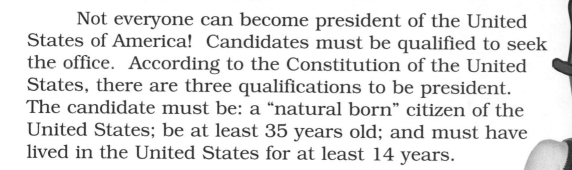

Not everyone can become president of the United States of America! Candidates must be qualified to seek the office. According to the Constitution of the United States, there are three qualifications to be president. The candidate must be: a "natural born" citizen of the United States; be at least 35 years old; and must have lived in the United States for at least 14 years.

Fast Fact!

You have to wait until you're eighteen to vote, but you don't have to wait until you're eighteen to learn about the candidates, form your own opinions, and think for yourself!

"Natural born" citizens are people born in the United States, or the children of U.S. citizens (such as soldiers or diplomats) who are temporarily living in another country.

Do the Math!

What year could you become president of the United States? **Use the space below to work out your answer!**

Hint: Take the year you were born and add 35. Remember that the presidential election is every four years. Since 2004 is an election year, what year could you become president of the United States?

Do the Math! _ _ _ _

+   35
—————

= —————

I can become president in _____ _____ _____ _____ !

8

Who's Next?

The Twentieth Amendment to the U.S. Constitution states that the vice president is to become president if the president dies. When William Henry Harrison died after only 30 days in office, Vice president John Tyler became president. At that time, it wasn't clearly stated in the Constitution that the vice president would become president, just acting president. Both houses of Congress had to pass resolutions declaring Tyler as president. If both the president and the vice president die, the order of presidential succession is as follows:

1. Speaker of the House
2. President Pro Tempore of the Senate
3. Secretary of State
4. Secretary of the Treasury
5. Secretary of Defense
6. Attorney General
7. Secretary of the Interior
8. Secretary of Agriculture
9. Secretary of Commerce
10. Secretary of Labor
11. Secretary of Health and Human Services
12. Secretary of Housing and Urban Development
13. Secretary of Transportation
14. Secretary of Energy
15. Secretary of Education
16. Secretary of Veterans Affairs

Fast Fact!

Inauguration Day was windy and cold, and William Henry Harrison refused to wear a coat or a hat. His speech was the longest in U.S. history, lasting nearly two hours! By the time the new president returned to the White House, he was chilled and utterly exhausted, and called for an alcohol rub. Exactly one month after he became president, Harrison died of pneumonia!

9

Succession Word Search

Find and circle the words listed in the Word Bank. Remember to cross off the words in the list as you find them!

Word Bank

Speaker • President • Secretary • State • Treasury • Defense • Attorney
Interior • Agriculture • Commerce • Labor • Health • Services • Housing
Development • Transportation • Energy • Education • Veterans

```
Q D T A L L R U T T R T T U F S V O G V U S
Y Q A L T M V B N U O N R V N D M K K W D T
L V D L Z W P E I U B E E B F Y T Y J S F V
H E D E C B D J U S A M A R C Z F J N C E G
Q F R E F I J V D F L P S F X L V A Z W T L
N E F U S E G A E P F O U T F C R F L J H C
T R T E T T N P W R Y L R Y M E L D U S O T
O T R A D L N S U U I E Y F T Q V S X D U H
U P C S T U U V E K B V S E C R E T A R Y O
O D L U R S C C T M E V E B C T X V Z W U U
Q W J H S P M A I M U D S H C O F S Y G R S
Z H W N O I T A T R O P S N A R T Z U Y T I
Y D I U V X Z E T I G S P E A K E R J L P N
J X V P C X H Y G C O A S C R O T M O D Z G
R T D P Y P U D A F N N E D E E T H M H C E
N W C H Z J K T L S C U C V H I I S E O H N
M J H X H E T J K Y F R I O L V J A Z V C T
S Z F C M O D J B S Q O V I J O L O I Q I V
E I P B R J L M Z G C Q R I E T S Y D O H L
I J D N R O I R E T N I E G H G Y S Y S S X
E I E Q D L P O I H E W S O K P N I L U D V
S Y G R E N E S R V G W X F H Q L J P H Z Q
```

10

Hitting the Campaign Trail

At each level of government, candidates for elective office are chosen using a variety of nominating methods. Individuals may seek nomination for national, state, and local office through:

- Caucus — a meeting of residents of an electoral district belonging to the same party to nominate and select candidates
- Direct primary — nomination system by which the people vote directly to select party nominees
- Nominating convention — a large meeting where delegates representing members of political parties get together and officially select nominees
- Petitions — document or list of signatures requesting a legislative or decision-making body to place a person on an election ballot

The two major political parties, Democrats and Republicans, use the national nominating convention to select presidential and vice-presidential candidates. State parties usually hold a series of local caucuses among rank-and-file members, culminating in a state convention where candidates receive the party's endorsement.

Be sure to vote for me!

Fill in the blanks using the words from above.

1. Citizens determine who will be a parties' candidates by voting in a _____.

2. Voters of a community get together to choose a candidate in a _____.

3. Political representatives gather to choose a candidate at a _____.

4. Voters of a community sign their name to support a candidate on a _____.

11

Political Symbols

Many different political parties exist in the United States today. A political party is a group of people who think alike about how to govern the nation. These organizations are usually very large.

Political parties want to get members elected to federal, state, and local offices so that their ideas will spread everywhere. Staff members in offices around the country help organize political campaigns to get people from their political party elected. They raise money to finance campaigns and recruit volunteers or staffers to help candidates win elections.

Currently, the two main political parties in the United States are the Republican and Democratic organizations. The Republican symbol is an elephant and the Democratic symbol is the donkey.

"The DEMOCRATIC Party can trace its roots back to Thomas Jefferson."

"The REPUBLICANS are also known as the GOP for Grand Old Party!"

VOTE

Color the symbols.

12

How Did He Get Elected?

At each level within the federal system, governing officials are either *elected* or *appointed*. Responsible citizens participate in elections at each level of government. On the national level, the president and vice president are elected using the Electoral College process. Members of Congress are also elected. Each state has two senators and at least one representative in Congress. Justices and Judges are appointed.

At the state level, each governor is elected.

Write the names of current elected officials for where you live here:

President:_____

Vice President:_____

Senator:_____

Senator:_____

Representative:_____

My State:_____

Governor:_____

Lt. Governor:_____

Legislator:_____

Legislator:_____

Fast Fact!

The media can be a resource to help you decide how to vote. Many newspapers have special sections that compare candidates in an election.

13

Making a Run for It!

At each level of government, candidates for elective office are chosen using a variety of nominating methods. Delegate conventions, caucuses, primaries, and self-announcement are the major methods of nominating candidates. At each level of government, political parties nominate candidates, conduct campaigns, and educate the public.

The two major political parties, the Democratic and Republican parties, dominate the electoral process. Both major political parties are organized to win elections, control government, and influence government policies. Each major political party seeks to define itself in a way that wins majority support while remaining committed to its core principles.

Number the steps in becoming a politician (running for office).

_____ 1. You are nominated by your party.

_____ 2. You join a political party.

_____ 3. You decide you want to get involved in government.

_____ 4. You talk to your friends and family about running for office.

_____ 5. You participate in debates and talk to voters.

Graduating from the Electoral College

The Electoral College was established by the U.S. Congress in 1789. It's not really a college at all, but "electors" (usually members of the major political parties) chosen from each state. The Electoral College process is used to select the president and vice president of the United States. The Electoral College works like this:

- Electors from each state are chosen by popular vote
- The electors meet to vote for the president and vice president positions
- The number of electors of each state is based on the state's Congressional representation

The requirements for a majority vote to win in the Electoral College favors a two-party system. The winner-take-all system leads to the targeting of large states for campaigning, although candidates must pay attention to small states whose electoral votes may make the difference in tight elections.

In the December following the presidential election, on a day set by law, the presidential electors in each state and the District of Columbia assemble. State electors usually meet in their state's capital. The electors then cast their ballots for president and vice president. Either by custom or, in a few states, by law, electors vote for their party's choices for the two offices. The lists of these elections are sent under seal to the president of the U.S. Senate and to the Administrator of General Services in Washington, D.C.

In January, at a joint session in the House of Representatives, the president of the Senate opens the certificates. Then one Democrat and one Republican from each house count the votes in the presence of both houses of Congress. The candidate who gets a majority of the electoral votes for president is elected.

15

Close Call!

The election in the fall of 2000 was a very close one. The country was divided almost evenly. All eyes were on the state of Florida. The popular vote was very close. The ballots in several Florida counties were recounted by machine and by hand — some counties more than once! In the end, George W. Bush won the presidency.

Election Results

CANDIDATE	ELECTORAL VOTES	STATES WON	VOTE %	VOTES
Bush	271	30	48%	50,456,169
Gore	266	21	48%	50,996,116

Examine the chart closely, then answer the following questions by writing B (for Bush) or G (for Gore) in the space provided.

_____ 1. Which candidate won the most electoral votes?

_____ 2. Which candidate won the most states?

_____ 3. Which candidate won the most votes?

_____ 4. Which candidate won the election?

Some people believe that because it is possible for a candidate to win an election *without having the majority of the popular vote*, that the candidate should not become president. Others argue that the Electoral College is the only way the candidates and the government give fair recognition to smaller states. Can you think of a way to make both sides happy?

16

Who Is Chad?

Who on earth is that "Chad" person we all heard about in the 2000 elections? Chad is a boy's name, but it also has another meaning. The word *chad* means those small pieces of paper that are formed when holes are punched through a punch card. Sometimes a chad does not completely come loose when a voter casts his or her ballot. *Oops!*

- A chad with only one loose corner was called a three-cornered chad.

- A chad with two loose corners was called a swinging chad.

- A chad with three loose corners was called a hanging chad.

- When it was clear that a voter tried to punch the card and there was a raised chad but none of the corners were loose, it was called a pregnant chad.

Below are two samples of kinds of ballots you might see when you vote. Try each one out, then discuss with your classmates or parents which was easiest, and why.

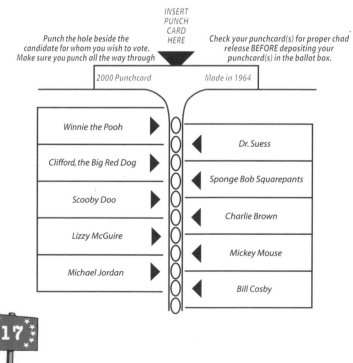

17

Get Involved!: Citizens' Role in Policy-Making

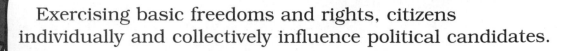

Exercising basic freedoms and rights, citizens individually and collectively influence political candidates.

Citizens can influence candidates by:
- Participating in politics (voting, campaigning)
- Expressing opinions (lobbying, demonstrating, writing letters)
- Participating in interest group activities

Match the special interest group with its concern

_____ 1. American Medical Association

_____ 2. National Organization for Women

_____ 3. Students Against Drunk Driving

_____ 4. American Association of Retired Persons

_____ 5. National Rifle Association

A. Opposes gun control

B. Opposes drunk driving

C. Protects doctors' interests

D. Promotes women's rights

E. Promotes rights of the elderly

Fast Fact!

Special interest groups often try to influence legislators' votes on certain bills. People called lobbyists, employed by interest groups, work in the national and state capitals, trying to convince legislators to vote for or against certain bills. A good lobbyist understands how government works and knows how to "push the buttons" of elected officials.

18

How Do You Decide?

Candidates for elective office use advertising to influence voters. Informed citizens evaluate information presented in political campaigns to make the best choices among candidates.

Responsible voters evaluate campaign speeches, literature, and advertisements for accuracy by:

- Separating fact from opinion
- Detecting bias
- Evaluating sources
- Identifying propaganda

Label each of the following statements with an F if it is a fact. Write an O if it is an opinion.

____ 1. The candidate lives in Kansas City.

____ 2. The candidate has a nice family.

____ 3. The candidate opposes the death penalty.

____ 4. The death penalty is wrong.

> Here are some advertising techniques commonly used by candidates to win voters over:
> - Patriotism: the candidate may pose with a flag in hand
> - Testimonials: people tell you good things about the candidate
> - "Warm fuzzies": the candidate is shown with his or her family or pet

Write B in front of each example of bias.

____ 5. The reporter who wrote the article has never met the candidate.

____ 6. The reporter is an employee of the candidate's opponent.

____ 7. The reporter who wrote an article about the candidate is the candidate's sister.

Just the Facts!

In an ideal world, the media are unbiased; they don't endorse a particular candidate or political party. Their main role is to report facts to the readers and viewers. However, most newspapers and television stations are owned by corporations who are interested in politics.

The media can be a resource to help you decide how to vote. Many newspapers have special sections that compare candidates in an election. The reporters who work for a newspaper have much more access to the facts about candidates than the ordinary citizen, and they can often be trusted to publish all the facts, not just what the candidate wants you to know!

Use the campaign poster and biography to write seven <u>facts</u> about the candidate.

1. _____

2. _____

3. _____

4. _____

5. _____

6. _____

7. _____

VOTE GAL O. PADE
for Governor !

★ INCREASED HEALTH CARE COVERAGE!
★ LOWER TAXES!
★ IMPROVED SCHOOLS!

Mrs. Gal O. Pade is running for Governor of our state. She has been in public service for the past 20 years. She has been a dedicated teacher, superintendent of schools, and mayor. Her record of excellence as a leader is unquestionable. She would like to be our state's leader now. Her character and experience far outshine her opponent's qualifications. Mrs. Gal O. Pade will make our state proud!

Influencing Voters

A number of factors influence public opinion during a political campaign.

Mass media coverage influences public opinion by selecting and controlling information relayed to the public. The media educates the public by presenting information. The media can influence the way people think and act by limiting the information to which the public is exposed. Public opinion is affected as much by the information the media chooses *not* to present as by what it *does* present. The media can influence election results by declaring premature results before voting polls close!

Scientific polling is used to measure public attitudes. People are randomly questioned to get their opinions on issues or candidates. Polling practices and questions can distort the results by favoring the candidate or issue of those commissioning the poll. Results can be used to influence voters and discourage other candidates from running.

Campaign advertisements can be used to persuade and/or mobilize the electorate. Most candidates use advertisements to educate voters about themselves and the issues they support. Candidates also use advertisements to encourage people to vote on Election Day. Some candidates use negative advertisements, or *mudslinging*, to emphasize their opponent's negative qualities and positions, rather than pointing out their own positive attributes.

Describe a recent local, state, or national campaign where public opinion was influenced by media coverage, campaign advertising, or public opinion polls.

Drawing the Lines

Changes in population and the resulting reapportionment have a political effect on legislative membership at the national, state, and local levels. The Constitution requires reapportionment of the House of Representatives seats every 10 years following the U.S. census.

Demographics can mean a change in:
(Check the boxes that apply.)

☐ Number of people   ☐ Number of pets

☐ Age of people   ☐ Favorite music

☐ Number of children   ☐ Age of children

Reapportionment of congressional, state, and local districts was controlled entirely by state and local laws until the U.S. Supreme Court ruled that unbalanced districts were unconstitutional. Several U.S. Supreme Court cases in the 1960s upheld the one person–one vote principle.

Word Definition

One person–one vote: reapportionment must be based on population balance. All congressional and state legislative districts must have equal populations within a state and cannot be structured unnaturally to favor or shut-out representation by political or ethnic groups.

Fast Fact! Demographics are characteristics of a population regarding its size, growth, density, distribution, and statistics regarding birth, marriage, disease, and death.

22

Gerry Who?

Word Definition

Gerrymander: the process of drawing district boundaries to benefit one political party or group of citizens. Named in honor of Governor Elbridge Gerry of Massachusetts, who redrew the state's districts to his own advantage in 1812.

Gerrymandering violates the U.S. Constitution if it violates the one person–one vote principle.

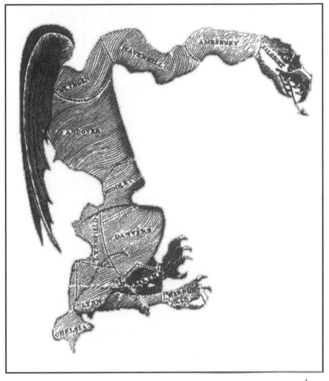

Gerrymander: *The Boston Weekly Messenger* published this drawing (by engraver Elkianah Tisdale) as THE GERRY-MANDER after the governor who had signed the redistricting bill.

What effect does reapportionment have on elections?

_____ It favors one political party or group.

_____ It makes elections fair.

How? _____

_____

_____

_____

Get Out and Vote!

The extent of engagement in a political campaign can be measured by voter turnout. There are several influences on voter turnout:

● Campaign issues — the matters or questions to be decided and voted on. People usually choose which candidate responds to campaign issues. If voters feel strongly *for* or *against* campaign issues, voter turnout will be high.

● Candidates — a person who runs for elective office. If voters strongly *support* or *oppose* a candidate, voter turnout will be high.

● Voter attitudes toward government — if voters are unhappy with politicians, candidates, and government, voter turnout will be low.

● Voter loyalty to political parties —voters who strongly support a political party are more likely to vote.

Check whether voter turnout will be high or low if...

High   Low

☐   ☐   1. Voters strongly support a candidate!

☐   ☐   2. Voters are unhappy with government.

☐   ☐   3. Voters strongly disagree with a candidate.

Your vote matters!

24

Who Does Vote?

More citizens vote in presidential elections than in other national, state, and local contests, but the percentage of Americans voting in presidential elections is going down. Education, age, and income are important factors in predicting which citizens will vote. Lack of interest, dissatisfaction, and the failure to meet voting requirements contribute to the decline in voting.

Check (✔) who will vote, or not!

	Vote	No Vote
1. I read all about the candidates.	☐	☐
2. I am six years-old.	☐	☐
3. Those candidates don't care about me.	☐	☐

The two major parties are made up of several interest groups. They recognize the importance of organizing campaigns that appeal to voters in the middle of the political spectrum. Their message usually does not move too far left or too far right of the political center.

Circle the group of people to which campaigns are designed to appeal.
(Hint: Campaign organizers want to get the most number of votes)

POLITICAL SPECTRUM

Extreme Left	Moderate Left	"Middle of the Road"	Moderate Right	Extreme Right

Voter Turnout In Recent Presidential Elections

ELECTION YEAR	CANDIDATES	VOTER PARTICIPATION (% OF VOTING-AGE POPULATION)
1932	Roosevelt-Hoover	52.4
1936	Roosevelt-Landon	56.0
1940	Roosevelt-Willkie	58.9
1944	Roosevelt-Dewey	56.0
1948	Truman-Dewey	51.1
1952	Eisenhower-Stevenson	61.6
1956	Eisenhower-Stevenson	59.3
1960	Kennedy-Nixon	62.8
1964	Johnson-Goldwater	61.9
1968	Nixon-Humphrey	60.9
1972	Nixon-McGovern	55.2
1976	Carter-Ford	53.5
1980	Reagan-Carter	54.0
1984	Reagan-Mondale	53.1
1988	Bush-Dukakis	50.2
1992	Clinton-Bush-Perot	55.9
1996	Clinton-Dole-Perot	49.0
2000	Bush-Gore	51.0

26

The Numbers are IN!

Use the table on the previous page to complete the chart. Draw dots on the chart to represent the voter participation, then connect the dots.

Voter Participation

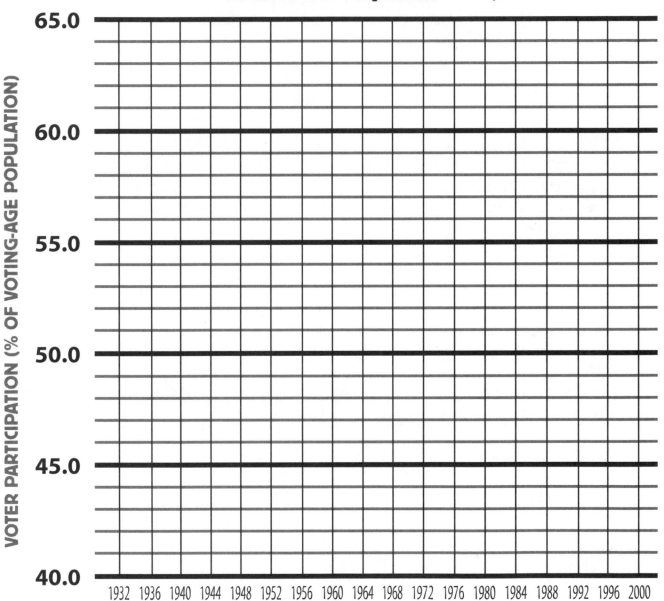

VOTER PARTICIPATION (% OF VOTING-AGE POPULATION)

65.0
60.0
55.0
50.0
45.0
40.0

1932 1936 1940 1944 1948 1952 1956 1960 1964 1968 1972 1976 1980 1984 1988 1992 1996 2000

PRESIDENTIAL ELECTION YEARS

27

The Candidate Goes to College

The Electoral College is used to select the president and vice president of the United States.

> The state of electors is chosen from each state by popular vote. The number of electors from each state equal the total U.S. senators and members of Congress from that state.

> The electors meet to vote for president and vice president. Electoral College members are supposed to reflect their states' voters' wishes.

> The winner-take-all custom leads to the targeting of large states for campaigning. Even if the popular vote in a state is close, the loser gets no electoral votes. In some states, electors are not required by law to vote the way the majority of their states' voters did, although they usually do.

> The requirement for a majority vote to win in the Electoral College favors a two-party system. To win, a candidate must receive at least a simple majority — 270 electoral votes.

If a candidate has 213 electoral votes, how many electoral votes will he or she need to win a presidential election?

Do the Math!

The candidate needs this many votes to win: _____

The candidate has this many votes: —   _____

The candidate needs this many votes: =   _____

Are You Informed?

How can you help make your community a better place?

1. Learn as much as you can about the economy, environment, education, poverty, crime, health care, foreign relations, and personal freedoms. Decide where you stand on each issue and which solutions you personally support.

2. Find out what federal district, state district, and voting precinct you live in. Find the location of your precinct voting place. Register to vote when you turn 18. If you are already 18, have you registered to vote yet?

3. Find out who your representatives are and write down their names, addresses, telephone numbers, and e-mail addresses. Include information for your city or town representatives, governor, state senator, state representative, U.S. Senators, U.S. Representative, and President of the United States.

4. Interact peacefully with people you don't agree with. A lot can be learned from a calm debate. Stay open-minded — seek new information and perspectives from people who don't agree with you.

Do the Math!

I will be eligible to vote on this date: _____

Hint: Take the year you were born and add the number 18. On your birthday in that year you will be eligible to vote!

Fast Fact!

You can find resource information at www.kids.gov.

Who Doesn't Vote?

Some citizens fail to vote. Citizens may choose not to vote because there is a lack of interest in the election. Sometimes citizens don't register to vote. Only citizens who are registered may vote (except in North Dakota!)

In many other democracies, at least 80 percent of all voters vote in national elections. Some nations get high voter turnouts by fining or even imprisoning citizens who do not vote!

Look at the pictures below. Show the sequence of a political campaign by putting the correct number in each box.

The Great Compromise

Creating a new constitution (in essence a new government) was not an easy task. Delegates from the large states disagreed with those from the small states about representation in the national legislature. The larger states favored the Virginia Plan, under which population would determine the number of representatives a state could send to the legislature. The small states supported the New Jersey Plan, which proposed that all the states would have an equal number of representatives.

The Connecticut delegates suggested a compromise that settled the problem. Their plan provided for equal representation in the Senate, along with representation in proportion to population in the House of Representatives. This proposal became known as the Connecticut Compromise or the Great Compromise.

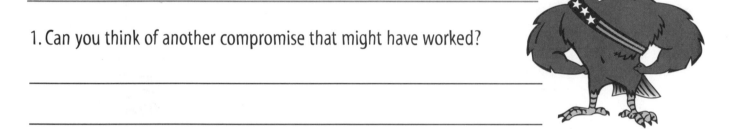

1. Can you think of another compromise that might have worked?

_____

_____

2. The number of votes each state has in the Electoral College is equal to its number of representatives in Congress. Some people do not like the Electoral College system. Recommend a solution to this problem.

_____

_____

3. Why was the Connecticut Compromise necessary? Describe its effect on American government.

_____

_____

31

Electoral Crossword

Use the Word Bank to solve the crossword puzzle.

I love crossword puzzles!

WORD BANK

ballot   candidate

delegate   election   majority

nominee   political party

poll   primary   vote

P O L I T I C A L P A R T Y

Vote for Uncle Sam!

The electorate are all the people who are registered to vote.

Presidential Dossier

The Secret Service is going digital, and they need your help!

Fill in the blanks with the facts you've learned about one of the presidents to get the Secret Service files up-to-date!

Fast Fact!

John Tyler had more children than any other president—15 altogether!

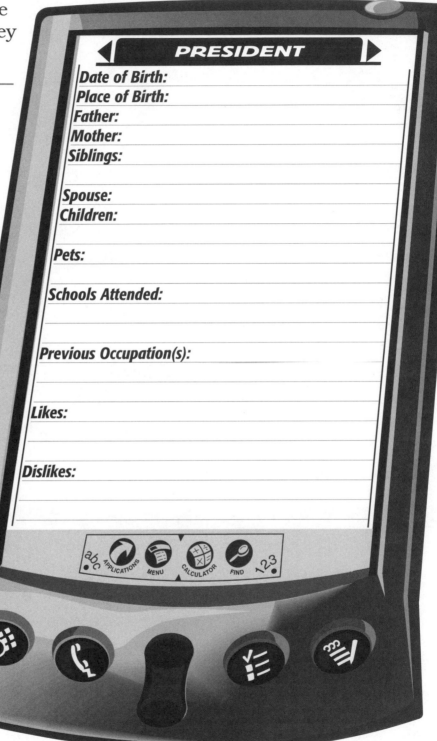

PRESIDENT

Date of Birth:

Place of Birth:

Father:

Mother:

Siblings:

Spouse:

Children:

Pets:

Schools Attended:

Previous Occupation(s):

Likes:

Dislikes:

abc APPLICATIONS MENU CALCULATOR FIND 123

33

What Does the Constitution...

For over 200 years, the Constitution of the United States of America has proved a remarkably flexible document. The government has changed, the times have changed, and voters have changed. Several changes have been made to the Constitution regarding voting.

● The Twelfth Amendment clarified the electoral procedure that had produced a confused result in 1800. It also redefined the vice-presidency in its relation to the presidency, and unofficially recognized the existence of political parties.

● The Fifteenth Amendment allowed people of all races to vote in presidential as well as other elections.

● The Seventeenth Amendment allowed voters in each state to elect their senators. Before this amendment, it was up to the state legislature to choose the senators for each state.

● The Nineteenth Amendment gave women the right to vote.

● The Twenty-second Amendment limited the length of time a person may serve as president.

● The Twenty-third Amendment gave citizens of the District of Columbia the right to vote for president and vice president.

● The Twenty-fourth Amendment makes "poll" taxes illegal. Poll taxes made it difficult or impossible for poor people to vote.

● The Twenty-sixth Amendment dropped the voting age from 21 to 18.

34

Say about Elections?

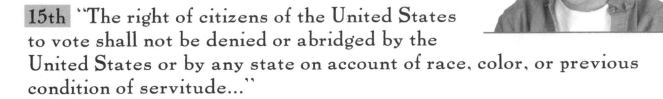

12th ... "the person having the greatest number of votes for president, shall be the president, if such number be a majority of the whole number of electors appointed..."

15th "The right of citizens of the United States to vote shall not be denied or abridged by the United States or by any state on account of race, color, or previous condition of servitude..."

17th "The Senate of the United States shall be composed of two Senators from each state, elected by the people thereof, for six years..."

19th "The right of citizens of the United States to vote shall not be denied or abridged by the United States or by any state on account of sex..."

22nd "No person shall be elected to the office of the president more than twice..."

23rd "The District [of Columbia] ... shall appoint ... a number of electors of president and vice president equal to the whole number of Senators and Representatives in Congress to which the District would be entitled if it were a state..."

24th "The right of citizens of the United States to vote in any ... election ... shall not be denied or abridged by the United States or any state by reason of failure to pay any poll tax or other tax..."

26th "The right of citizens of the United States, who are 18 years of age or older, to vote, shall not be denied or abridged by the United States or any state on account of age..."

35

Election Day Calendar

Every four years, a very special thing happens in the United States. Citizens of the United States elect a new president! This special day is called Election Day. Election Day is the Tuesday after the first Monday in November.

On each calendar, circle the Tuesday that would be a national election day.

SUN	MON	TUES	WEDS	THURS	FRI	SAT
	1	2	3	4	5	6
7	8	9	10	11	12	13
14	15	16	17	18	19	20
21	22	23	24	25	26	27
28	29	30				

SUN	MON	TUES	WEDS	THURS	FRI	SAT
				1	2	3
4	5	6	7	8	9	10
11	12	13	14	15	16	17
18	19	20	21	22	23	24
25	26	27	28	28	30	

SUN	MON	TUES	WEDS	THURS	FRI	SAT
			1	2	3	4
5	6	7	8	9	10	11
12	13	14	15	16	17	18
19	20	21	22	23	24	25
26	27	28	29	30		

SUN	MON	TUES	WEDS	THURS	FRI	SAT
1	2	3	4	5	6	7
8	9	10	11	12	13	14
15	16	17	18	19	20	21
22	23	24	25	26	27	28
29	30					

Fast Fact!

Each state picks its own election days for state and local elections, but election day for national elections is designated by law as the Tuesday after the first Monday in November in even-numbered years.

36

Recipe for an Election

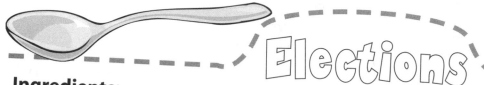

In a way, an election is a little bit like cooking. Here is a recipe for you to chew on while learning about presidential elections.

Elections

Ingredients:

2 candidates (Add more candidates to taste)
5–6 million grassroots workers
8–12 key issues
3–4 large campaigns

12–14 heated debates
5–6 attack ads (optional)
1 Electoral College
537 electoral votes

Preparation time: 18 months, **Serves:** 281,421,906

Cooking Directions: This recipe can be adjusted for your own election. However, at *least* two candidates are necessary to have an election. Some people prefer to add in a dark horse candidate to make the flavor of the election more interesting. Occasionally a candidate can find himself or herself in hot water. This can also add flavor to the recipe.

Sprinkle in key issues to taste. Check progress when the last ballot is cast on Election Day. Continue stirring the pot until the Electoral College decides it's done. (In some cases, it may take the Supreme Court to decide when the election is done!) Be careful — too many cooks can spoil the pot!

Note: In the case of an incumbent who loses an election, don't let it spoil — it may become a lame duck!

This recipe serves a large number of people because it is designed to serve the population of the United States. Attack ads are optional because they can leave a bad taste in your mouth!

37

The First Woman President

When will we get one? It may be as soon as the next election, but until a woman becomes the President of the United States we will continue to ask, "Who will it be?" Even though there has not been a woman president — yet — the first woman president will have many female political leaders to look up to!

● In 1917, Jeanette Rankin of Montana was the first woman elected to the U.S. House of Representatives.

● Shirley Chisholm was the first African American woman elected to the U.S. House of Representatives, in 1968.

● In 1974, Ella T. Grasso was elected the governor of Connecticut. (Some women had been appointed governor after their governor-husbands died, but she was first to be elected on her own merit.)

● Women have served as mayor of major U.S. cities, including Atlanta, Chicago, Oklahoma City, San Francisco, and Washington D.C.

38

Fast Fact!

Women Who Ran for President... So Far!

1872 Victoria Woodhull

1884 Belva Lockwood

1964 Margaret Chase Smith

1972 Shirley Chisholm

1987 Patricia Schroeder

The Candidates

Read over the following possible *pretend* candidates for presidential office and see who you might be willing to vote for if they actually ran! Make your choice below. If real candidates' names were substituted, how do you think that might influence your vote?

Name: Pat P. Politix
Platform: Peace and prosperity for all!

Name: Lefty Right
Platform: Please all the people all the time!

Name: Smart T. Pants
Platform: Year round school for all!

Name: Sunshine Tomorrow
Platform: Tax cuts for everyone!

Name: Iam Normal
Platform: Let's have as little change as possible!

Name: V. For Me
Platform: I'll keep my promises — I promise!

SPEECH! SPEECH!

Pretend you are running for the office of president of the United States. Write a short campaign on a separate piece of paper, explaining your platform and why you think you are the best person for the job.

39

Campaign Button

Campaign buttons have been a big part of presidential elections for many years. Sometimes buttons have simple designs with just the candidate's name printed on them. Other times campaign buttons have catchy slogans such as "I like Ike."

Today, candidates still pass out campaign buttons. Many people collect campaign buttons. The most popular are ones with slogans and pictures.

Pretend that you are running for president. Design your own campaign button. Be sure to include a slogan as well as a picture.

Other Catchy Campaign Slogans:

1840 William Henry Harrison — Tippecanoe and Tyler too

1864 Abraham Lincoln — Don't swap horses in the middle of the stream

1928 Herbert Hoover — A chicken in every pot and a car in every garage

1976 Jimmy Carter — Not just peanuts

1996 Bill Clinton — Building a bridge to the 21st century

2000 George W. Bush — No child left behind

40

Campaign Fun

FOOD

PARTY

The most exciting thing about presidential elections is all the fun events. Candidates often host barbecues, dinner parties, and pig pickings. Candidates show up in commercials, debates, and make special appearances on TV shows. The next president might also show up at a parade, fair, or a popular restaurant.

Presidential hopefuls have often made promotional tours by train, where the candidate stops in towns along a route to make speeches where crowds eagerly wait to hear details about the party platform. Campaigners always try to make voters feel special by shaking hands or holding and kissing little babies.

Grassroots efforts to raise popularity for candidates have always been important. Without the support of voters at the local level, a candidate will never succeed. It takes a lot of work to win an election. Some people are paid to work on presidential election campaigns, but most of them are volunteers. Volunteers are the heart of a grassroots organization. Without them a candidate could not get elected President.

Check the box next to ways you can help with grassroots organization.

☐ Volunteers can pass out fliers.

☐ Volunteers can answer telephones.

☐ Volunteers can raise money to help support the campaign.

☐ Volunteers can tell others about their favorite candidate.

Fast Fact!

In 1928, presidential candidate Frank T. Johns heroically jumped in a river to save a drowning boy. Sadly, the boy and the candidate both drowned!

41

Presidential Election Winners

Here is a list of presidential election winners — so far. The next presidential election is in 2004. Will we have a new president, or will the incumbent win? Only time (and the Electoral College) will tell.

PRESIDENT	YEARS	PARTY	PRESIDENT	YEARS	PARTY
George Washington	1789–1797	Federalist	Chester A. Arthur	1881–1885	Republican
John Adams	1797–1801	Federalist	Grover Cleveland	1885–1889	Democratic
Thomas Jefferson	1801–1809	Democratic/Republican	Benjamin Harrison	1889–1893	Republican
			Grover Cleveland	1893–1897	Democratic
James Madison	1809–1817	Democratic/Republican	William McKinley	1897–1901	Republican
			Theodore Roosevelt	1901–1909	Republican
James Monroe	1817–1825	Democratic/Republican	William Howard Taft	1909–1913	Republican
			Woodrow Wilson	1913–1921	Democratic
John Quincy Adams	1825–1829	Democratic/Republican	Warren G. Harding	1921–1923	Republican
			Calvin Coolidge	1923–1929	Republican
Andrew Jackson	1829–1837	Democratic	Herbert Hoover	1929–1933	Republican
Martin Van Buren	1837–1841	Democratic	Franklin D. Roosevelt	1933–1945	Democratic
William Henry Harrison	1841	Whig	Harry S. Truman	1945–1953	Democratic
John Tyler	1841–1845	Whig	Dwight D. Eisenhower	1953–1961	Republican
James K. Polk	1845–1849	Democratic	John F. Kennedy	1961–1963	Democratic
Zachary Taylor	1849–1850	Whig	Lyndon B. Johnson	1963–1969	Democratic
Millard Fillmore	1850–1853	Whig	Richard M. Nixon	1969–1974	Republican
Franklin Pierce	1853–1857	Democratic	Gerald R. Ford	1974–1977	Republican
James Buchanan	1857–1861	Democratic	James (Jimmy) Carter	1977–1981	Democratic
Abraham Lincoln	1861–1865	Republican	Ronald Reagan	1981–1989	Republican
Andrew Johnson	1865–1869	Republican	George Bush	1989–1993	Republican
Ulysses S. Grant	1869–1877	Republican	Bill Clinton	1993–2001	Democratic
Rutherford B. Hayes	1877–1881	Republican	George W. Bush	2001–	Republican
James A. Garfield	1881	Republican			

Who will be next?

Presidential Elections Quiz

1. How many electoral votes are required to win an election?
   - A 27
   - B 270
   - C 537
   - D 281,421,906

2. The Tuesday after the first Monday in November is called —
   - A Election Day
   - B Thanksgiving
   - C Happy Birthday
   - D Leap Year

3. "Electors" (usually members of the major political parties) chosen from each state are called —
   - A Electoral College
   - B Electoral Candidates
   - C Presidential Candidates
   - D College Graduates

4. What are the requirements to become president?
   - A Must be a natural born citizen
   - B Must be at least 35 years old
   - C Must have lived in the United States for at least 14 years
   - D All of these

5. Who is next in line if the president dies?
   - A Speaker of the House
   - B Vice president
   - C President Pro Tempore of the Senate
   - D Secretary of State

6. A document or list of signatures that makes a request of a legislative body is a —
   - A Caucus
   - B Direct Primary
   - C Nominating Convention
   - D Petition

7. Which symbol represents the Democratic Party?
   - A Elephant
   - B Monkey
   - C Donkey
   - D Stars and Stripes

8. Which symbol represents the Republican Party?
   - A Elephant
   - B Monkey
   - C Donkey
   - D Stars and Stripes

9. Characteristics of a population regarding its size, growth, density is called —
   - A Special graphics
   - B Awesome graphics
   - C Demographics
   - D Shady graphics

10. Local people who work together on a campaign are called the —
    - A Deep roots
    - B Grassroots
    - C Ancient roots
    - D Root cellar

Great job! You're on your way to the presidency!

About the Author

Carole Marsh is the founder and CEO of Gallopade International. She travels throughout the United States and around the world to research her books. In 1979 Marsh was named Communicator of the Year for her corporate communications work with major national and international corporations. Today, Gallopade International is widely recognized as a leading source of educational materials. Marsh and Gallopade were recipients of the 2002 Teachers' Choice Award. Marsh has written more than 16 Carole Marsh Mysteries™.

"When I was in school, we were required to take a 'civics' course in 7th grade. That was pretty much the beginning and end of our education on how to be a productive citizen. I believe kids should be introduced to so-called 'hard' subjects at an early age so that they can keep up with the dinner table conversation and classroom current event discussions on what is happening in their state."

"Kids, you can do your part by at least reading or listening to or watching the news about the daily governmental affairs. Ask questions about what interests you, even if it's only the silly, strange, or dumb stuff — there's plenty of that in politics!"

Ms. Marsh welcomes correspondence from her readers. You can e-mail her at carole@gallopade.com, visit the gallopade.com website, or write to her in care of Gallopade International, P.O. Box 2779, Peachtree City, Georgia, 30269 USA.

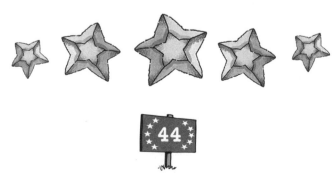

Bibliography

BOOKS

The Buck Stops Here: The Presidents of the United States
by Alice Provensen

Facts and Fun About the Presidents
by George Sullivan

Politics for Dummies
by Ann Delaney

Real Life Dictionary of American Politics:
What They're Saying and What It Really Means
by Kathleen Thompson Hill and Gerald N. Hill

INTERNET WEBSITES

The White House Project
http://www.thewhitehouseproject.org

Close Up Foundation
www.closeup.org

Presidential Classroom
www.presidentialclassroom.org

Junior State of America
www.jsa.org

Washington Workshops Foundation
www.workshops.org

Congressional Youth Leadership Council
www.cylc.org

Taking It Global
www.takingitglobal.org

45

Election Glossary

absentee ballot: you can vote by mail if you are out of the state on Election Day

accountability: elected officials must prove they are doing the job the people elected them to do

amendment: alteration of or addition to a bill, constitution, etc.; a change made by correction, addition, or deletion

apathy: lack of interest in anything; as in "The voters were apathetic because there were no important issues."

ballot: a piece of paper you use to vote on anonymously that will be counted confidentially

bicameral: legislature with two houses or chambers

bill: written proposal to change or create a new law

bipartisan: when people from two political parties work together to get something done, such as a bill passed into law

bureaucrat: person who gets into office, then just does a so-so job instead of working for improvement

caucus: comes from a Native American word that means to speak or to counsel; in politics it is a meeting of members of a political party to choose candidates or determine policy

census: an official count of the population with details on age, sex, occupation, etc.

coalition: a group of people who work together to achieve a particular goal in government

dark horse: an unknown candidate who sometimes surprises people by winning an election

direct primary: nomination system by which the people vote directly to select party nominees

electorate: all people who are registered to vote

federalism: power is divided and shared between the federal government and individual states

Election Glossary

filibuster: a long-winded speech given to delay the passage of a bill

franchise: the right to vote

gerrymander: when a legislative district is created to include people in favor of a certain candidate

grassroots: local people who work together on a campaign

incumbent: a person already in office who runs for that office again

lame duck: an incumbent office holder who has lost the election, but has not officially left office; "lame ducks" sometimes seem less powerful because he or she will soon leave office

nominating convention: a large meeting where delegates representing members of political parties get together and officially select nominees

one person–one vote: reapportionment must be based on population balance

petition: document or list of signatures requesting a legislative or decision-making body to place a person on an election ballot

primary: (see direct primary)

propaganda: ideas spread to influence people to feel or vote a certain way

soft money: money that can't be given legally to a federal candidate; these contributions must be donated to state and national parties rather than directly to the candidates

suffrage: the right to vote in political or public elections, often associated with women's suffrage

underdog: candidate for office who is not believed to have much of a chance to win—but sometimes does!

voter registration: document to be filled out ahead of time before you can vote

write-in candidate: a person you vote for by writing in their name on the ballot

Index

48